Genetics

Titles in the KidHaven Science Library include:

The KidHaven Science Library

Genetics

by Buffy Silverman

KIDHAVEN
PRESS™

THOMSON
——★——™
GALE

San Diego • Detroit • New York • San Francisco • Cleveland
New Haven, Conn. • Waterville, Maine • London • Munich

© 2004 by KidHaven Press. KidHaven Press is an imprint of The Gale Group, Inc., a division of Thomson Learning, Inc.

KidHaven™ and Thomson Learning™ are trademarks used herein under license.

For more information, contact
KidHaven Press
27500 Drake Rd.
Farmington Hills, MI 48331-3535
Or you can visit our Internet site at http://www.gale.com

LIBRARY OF CONGRESS CATALOGING-IN-PUBLICATION DATA

Silverman, Buffy.
    Genetics : by Buffy Silverman.
        v. cm. — (KidHaven science library)
Includes bibliographical references and index.
Contents: The inheritance of traits—Genetics and medicine—DNA fingerprinting—Cloning.
    ISBN 0-7377-1014-4 (hardback)
    1. Genetics—Juvenile literature. [1. Genetics.] I. Title. II. Series.
    QH437.5.S57 2004
    576—dc21
                                   2003007299

Printed in the United States of America

Contents

Chapter 1

The Inheritance of Traits

Genetics is the science of how living things pass on characteristics from one generation to the next. Long ago people noticed that children often looked like their parents, and concluded that many physical features are passed on from parents to children. Red-haired parents often had red-haired children. Long-haired dogs frequently gave birth to long-haired puppies. Yellow-flowered plants made seeds that usually grew into yellow-flowered plants.

People used this knowledge to try to improve the animals that helped them do their work. If a farmer needed strong horses to plow his fields, he chose a strong male horse to mate with a strong female horse. This made it more likely that the female horse gave birth to colts that grew into strong horses.

People also paid attention to the size and taste of the food they grew. If a farmer found apple trees that grew sweet-tasting apples, he tried to grow more trees with sweet apples. He transferred pollen from flowers growing on a sweet-apple tree to the flowers of another sweet-apple tree. The transfer of pollen from one flower to another is known as cross-pollination. Cross-pollination causes a flower to grow into a fruit with seeds. When the newly pollinated flowers grew into apples, the farmer collected the seeds inside. The trees that grew from those seeds were likely to make sweet-flavored apples.

While animal and plant breeders were success-ful some of the time, they noticed that some phys-ical features, or **traits**, were not always passed on

Identical twin girls play in the back of the family car. Identical twins have the same features because they have the same genes.

to offspring. Some offspring had traits that were different from those of either parent.

Gregor Mendel, Father of Modern Genetics

Gregor Mendel, an Austrian monk who lived from 1822 to 1884, wondered how offspring received, or **inherited**, traits from their parents. After raising pea plants for several years, Mendel found seven traits that were passed on from one generation of pea plants to the next. The traits were flower color, seed color, pod color, seed shape, pod shape, stem length, and flower position. Each trait had two forms. For example, pea plants had either purple flowers or white flowers. They had round seeds or wrinkled seeds. They had green pods or yellow pods. Mendel experimented with traits by mating plants with different forms, and he found some surprising results.

First, Mendel used pollen from plants with white flowers to pollinate plants with purple flowers. He collected the pea seeds that grew from the purple-

Gregor Mendel pioneered genetic research in plants.

flowered plants and planted them. All of these plants grew purple flowers. The white-flower trait seemed to have disappeared.

Next, Mendel crossed these new purple-flowered plants with each other. When he planted their seeds, three-fourths grew into plants with purple flowers and one-fourth grew into plants with white flowers. The white-flower trait had reappeared.

Dominant and Recessive Genes

Mendel concluded that a pea plant with purple flowers had a stronger influence in determining what color flowers its offspring would grow. A pea plant with white flowers had less influence in determining flower color. He called the purple flower trait **dominant**. He called the white flower trait **recessive**.

For each of the seven traits that he tested, Mendel found similar results. He cross-pollinated plants having round seeds with those having wrinkled seeds. All of their offspring had round seeds. When these round-seeded plants were crossed with each other, three-fourths of the plants that grew had round seeds and one-fourth had wrinkled seeds.

From his many years of experimenting with pea plants, Mendel concluded that each pea plant had two hereditary "factors" for each trait. Scientists now call Mendel's "factors" **genes**.

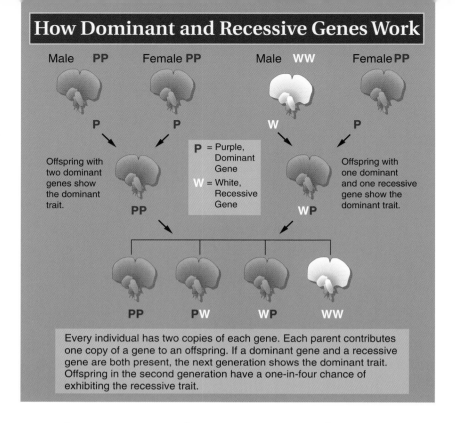

How Dominant and Recessive Genes Work

Male PP   Female PP   Male WW   Female PP

P   P   W   P

Offspring with two dominant genes show the dominant trait.

PP

P = Purple, Dominant Gene

W = White, Recessive Gene

Offspring with one dominant and one recessive gene show the dominant trait.

WP

PP   PW   WP   WW

Every individual has two copies of each gene. Each parent contributes one copy of a gene to an offspring. If a dominant gene and a recessive gene are both present, the next generation shows the dominant trait. Offspring in the second generation have a one-in-four chance of exhibiting the recessive trait.

Each parent contributes one copy of each gene to its offspring. A pea flower will be purple if the plant inherits one or two copies of the "purple" gene, because the purple form is dominant. For a pea flower to be white, it must inherit two copies of the recessive "white" gene, one from each parent. Similarly, a pea plant with one or two copies of the dominant "round" gene will have round seeds. A pea plant must have two copies of the recessive "wrinkled" gene for its seeds to be wrinkled.

Genes in Cells

When Gregor Mendel published his findings in 1868, other scientists did not believe his conclusions. But today scientists agree with Mendel. They know that a pair of genes has the information for a trait, and each parent contributes one part of the pair to its offspring.

The genes of a living organism are in its cells. Plants, animals, and all other living things are made up of cells. Cells are too small to be seen with the eye, but they can be viewed with a microscope. Some organisms have only one cell. Complex organisms, like horses or people, are made of billions of cells. Every cell within a living organism has a complete copy of its genes.

Chromosomes

Most cells have a control center, called the nucleus. Inside the nucleus are rod-shaped structures called **chromosomes** that contain the genes. There are two copies of each type of chromosome. One chromosome of each pair comes from each parent. Different kinds of plants and animals have different numbers of chromosomes. Some scorpions have 2 pairs of chromosomes, onions have 8 pairs, and certain kinds of hermit crabs have 127 pairs of chromosomes. People have 23 pairs of chromosomes, or 46 chromosomes total.

Each chromosome is made of a long molecule called **DNA** (deoxyribonucleic acid). A gene is a section of a DNA molecule. Scientists believe that there are about forty thousand genes in a complete set of human chromosomes.

Inside a Cell

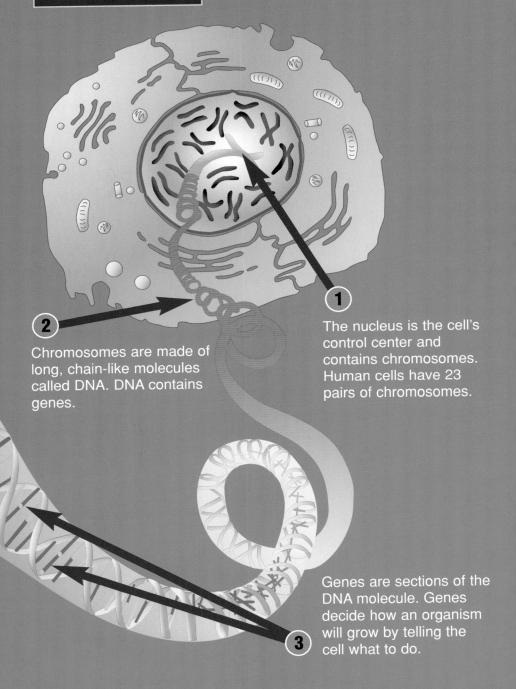

2 Chromosomes are made of long, chain-like molecules called DNA. DNA contains genes.

1 The nucleus is the cell's control center and contains chromosomes. Human cells have 23 pairs of chromosomes.

3 Genes are sections of the DNA molecule. Genes decide how an organism will grow by telling the cell what to do.

Genes tell a cell how to build body structures and how to make chemicals that control chemical reactions inside the cell. By controlling each individual cell, the genes help govern how a living organism grows, what it looks like, and its day-to-day activity.

Copying Genes

A living organism makes new cells in order to grow, to replace old cells, or to repair an injury. A single cell divides in two to make two new cells. Before a cell divides, each of its chromosomes makes a copy of itself. Once it has divided, each new cell has a complete set of chromosomes.

Human sperm swim toward an egg. One sperm joins with the egg to create new life.

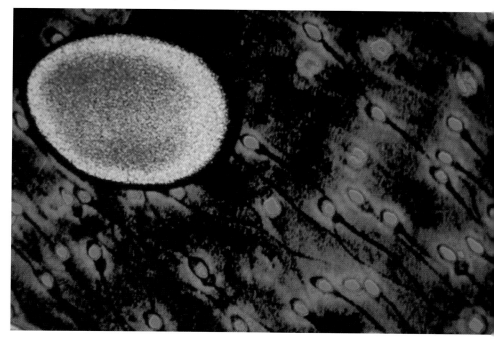

When a living organism reproduces, or creates a new life, its offspring must have the same number of chromosomes as the parent. Most animals and all flowering plants make special cells for sexual reproduction. Animal fathers make cells called sperm. Animal mothers make eggs. When a sperm and egg unite, a new individual begins to grow.

Cell Division

Sperm and egg cells are made by a different kind of cell division. Pairs of chromosomes line up and then separate. The sperm and eggs that result have one of each kind of chromosome, or half the total number of chromosomes. Human sperm and egg cells have twenty-three chromosomes. When a human sperm joins with a human egg, the two sets of chromosomes combine. It makes a new cell with twenty-three pairs of chromosomes, or forty-six chromosomes in all. This new cell divides and grows into a human baby. Thus, a baby inherits its parents' genes from the chromosomes in the sperm and egg. The information that tells it how to grow and develop is contained in these genes.

Chapter 2

Genetics and Human Health

The genes that children inherit from their parents determine whether they will grow short or tall, have blond hair or brown, or run fast or slow. People's genes also control whether or not they will get certain diseases. There are over four thousand diseases that people inherit from their parents. Down syndrome, Huntington's disease, Tay-Sachs disease, cystic fibrosis, and sickle-cell anemia are a few of the many inherited diseases.

Genes have the instructions that tell cells how to work. For a human to grow and be healthy, all of its cells need a correct copy of its genes. When there is an error in the genes, cells do not have the right instructions. With the wrong instructions, a disease may develop.

Mutations

Every time a cell divides, it copies its DNA. Usually a cell copies its DNA correctly. But sometimes a mistake is made. Cells are able to fix many of the copying mistakes made during cell division. If a

Down Syndrome is one of over four thousand genetic diseases that people inherit from their parents.

cell cannot repair the DNA, the mistake is passed on to new cells during cell division. A mistake in a gene that is passed on to other cells is called a **mutation**.

Genes contain chemicals called **nitrogen bases**. The information in a gene is determined by the order of these bases. The nitrogen bases for each gene are like letters that spell out instructions for a cell, including how to build a protein. The order and number of nitrogen bases is different for different genes.

When a mutation occurs, the arrangement of nitrogen bases on a gene changes. Sometimes an extra nitrogen base is added, and sometimes a base is left out. Sometimes one base is substituted for another.

A mutation changes the instructions that a gene has for a cell. Some mutations do not harm a living thing, but most make it hard for cells to do their jobs.

Some mutations happen during an individual's life. Genes can change when they are exposed to dangerous chemicals or too much sunlight. Only the cells that are damaged have the changed genes. Skin cancer is a disease that occurs when genes in

Former president George Bush was treated for skin cancer on his face. Genes in the skin cells mutated because they were exposed to too much sunlight.

skin cells are harmed by too much sunlight. Skin cells with gene mutations rapidly divide, producing more mutated skin cells. The cancerous group of cells overgrows the normal cells that surround it. This kind of mutation is not passed on to offspring.

Other mutations are inherited from parents. If a sperm or egg cell has a gene with a mutation, then a child will inherit the mutation. All of the child's cells will have the altered gene.

Cystic Fibrosis: An Inherited Genetic Disease

Cystic fibrosis is one of the most common genetic diseases that shortens a person's life. People with cystic fibrosis have thick, sticky mucus that clogs their lungs and other organs. This can make it hard to breathe and to digest food. There are thirty thousand people with cystic fibrosis in the United States.

Cystic fibrosis is a recessive disease. A person gets this disease only if he or she inherits copies of the mutated cystic fibrosis gene from both parents. A person with one normal gene and one defective gene has no sign of cystic fibrosis. That person is called a carrier. One in thirty-one Americans carries the cystic fibrosis gene.

Suppose two cystic fibrosis carriers have a child. Each parent has one copy of the defective gene and one copy of the normal gene. There is a one-in-four chance that the child will inherit two defective genes and have cystic fibrosis. There is a two-in-four chance that the child will be a carrier of the disease, and a one-in-four chance that the child will be a normal noncarrier.

Genes tell cells how to build **proteins**. A person with two copies of the defective cystic fibrosis gene does not have the right instructions to make a protein called CFTR. Without the correct CFTR protein, cells do not pump salt and water correctly. Mucus becomes thick, sticky, and hard to move.

Scientists have found 1,000 different mutations that cause cystic fibrosis. The cystic fibrosis gene has 250,000 pairs of nitrogen bases. In the most common mutation, three of the gene's 250,000

A therapist helps a cystic fibrosis patient inhale a spray that allows her to breathe. She has a defective gene that causes her body to produce too much mucus.

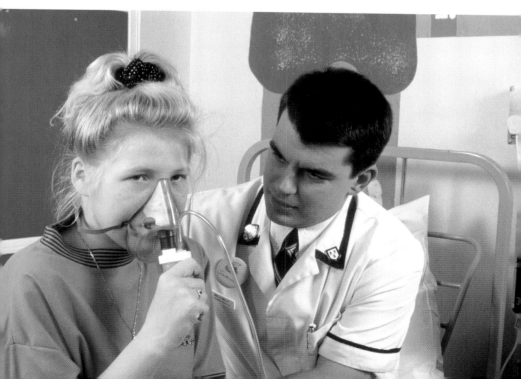

base pairs are missing. This means that the CFTR protein is missing just one tiny section, called an amino acid. Without that amino acid, the CFTR protein does not work properly.

Sickle-Cell Anemia

Sickle-cell anemia is a genetic disease that affects one out of every 625 African Americans. Hemoglobin, a protein in red blood cells, carries oxygen to all organs of the body. People with sickle-cell anemia make defective hemoglobin, which makes their red blood cells hard and pointed instead of soft and round. These cells get stuck in small blood vessels and cannot carry enough oxygen to the body. Sickle-cell anemia causes muscle cramps, shortness of breath, tiredness, and sometimes heart failure.

Sickle-cell anemia is a recessive disease. Usually a carrier, a person with one normal gene and one sickle-cell gene, does not show signs of sickle-cell anemia. If two carriers of the sickle-cell gene have a child, there is a one-in-four chance that the child will have the disease. There is a two-in-four chance that the child will be a carrier of the disease and a one-in-four chance that the child will be a normal noncarrier.

Gene Therapy

Someday scientists hope to be able to treat people with genetic diseases by using **gene therapy**. They

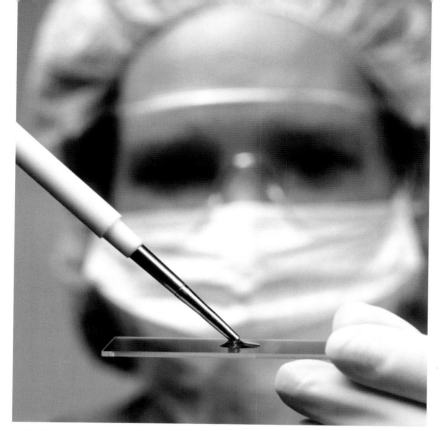

A lab worker prepares a blood sample to test for genetic diseases such as sickle-cell anemia.

will give people copies of the healthy gene they are missing. The first step is to find the defective gene that causes a disease. Scientists have done this for many diseases, including cystic fibrosis and sickle-cell anemia.

Next, the "normal" gene is made in a laboratory using state-of-the-art biotechnology. After it is made, the healthy gene must be delivered to a person's diseased cells. Healthy genes can be put inside viruses that bring the genes to damaged cells. Scientists are also compressing entire strands

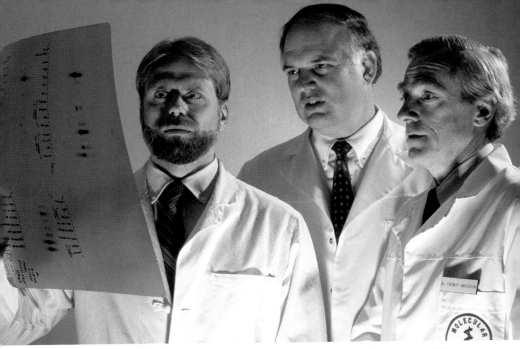

Gene therapists study a DNA chart. Gene therapy will one day be used to treat patients with genetic diseases.

of DNA so they are tiny enough to enter a cell's nucleus.

The aim of gene therapy is for the healthy genes to tell the cells to produce normal proteins. Researchers have given people with cystic fibrosis healthy genes in some of their lung cells and nasal passages. These genes tell cells to make the CFTR protein so the person can breathe easier. Someday gene therapy may be able to cure people with cystic fibrosis and sickle-cell anemia.

In the future, genetic diseases may be cured before babies are born. A parent who is a carrier of a disease may be able to have healthy genes inserted in sperm or egg cells. Then the baby will be born without the genetic disease.

Chapter 3

Solving Crimes with DNA

All people have fingerprints. The pattern of whorls and ridges on the tip of a person's fingers are unique, so no two people have the same fingerprints. When someone touches an object, a mark is left that shows a person's fingerprints. Police look for fingerprints left at a crime scene. When a person is accused of a crime, the fingerprints are shown as evidence that the person was at the crime scene.

Today police also look for a different kind of fingerprint when a crime occurs. They look for evidence of a person's DNA to prove that someone was at a crime scene. Just as no two people have the same fingerprints, the genes that make up a person's DNA are unique. Unless a person has an identical twin, no one else has the exact same DNA.

Every cell in a person's body has a copy of his or her DNA. A strand of hair, a spot of blood, or dead skin cells on clothing have copies of a person's DNA. DNA can be identified from the bones or teeth of a skeleton. Even saliva on the back of a licked postage stamp contains a person's genes. Scientists use the term **DNA fingerprint** to describe the information they find when they analyze DNA from materials like hair or skin cells. They then use the information to identify people.

DNA fingerprints are becoming the most accepted method of identifying people. Police and FBI labs use them to show if a person could or could not have committed a crime. Soldiers in the U.S. armed services have DNA fingerprints taken so they can be identified if they are killed in

A lab technician opens a sample of DNA from a crime scene. Experts use DNA to identify criminals.

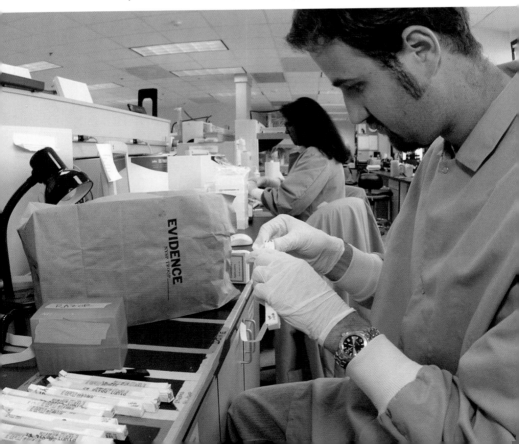

action. DNA fingerprints are used to prove if someone is the father of a child.

What Is a DNA Fingerprint?

The DNA molecule is shaped like a twisted ladder, with pairs of nitrogen bases connecting the two sides of the ladder. There are four different nitrogen bases in a DNA molecule. The four bases are adenine, thymine, guanine, and cytosine, usually abbreviated as A, T, G, and C. An adenine (A) base always connects to a thymine (T) base. A guanine (G) base connects to a cytosine (C) base.

A DNA fingerprint shows the sequence of nitrogen bases. The sequence of bases is different for different people. Using DNA fingerprints, the sequences of bases from different people can be compared.

When a DNA fingerprint is made, only some of a person's DNA is examined. Because a person's DNA is made up of 3.3 billion base pairs, it is not possible to look at all the DNA. Instead, scientists look at small sections of DNA. They choose sections that vary a lot among different people. Because scientists have studied how much these sections of DNA vary, they can say how likely it is that one person will have a certain DNA sequence. By looking at several DNA sequences, they can make prints that are most likely to identify a person.

This colorful model shows strands of DNA wrapped together in a twisted ladder known as a double helix.

Unlike a regular fingerprint, a DNA fingerprint does not absolutely prove that a DNA sample came from a certain person. It can prove that a sample is highly likely to have come from someone, or that it definitely did not come from someone.

Suppose a police detective finds a spot of blood on the shirt of someone accused of murder. The detective sends the shirt to a laboratory. A sample of blood from the person who was murdered is also labeled and sent.

At the laboratory, a technician makes a DNA fingerprint of the blood from the suspect's shirt and the blood from the victim. The technician compares the two DNA fingerprints. If they are different, then the blood on the shirt definitely did not come from the victim. If the DNA fingerprint is the same, it is highly probable that the blood spot is from the person who was killed and that the suspect was present at the murder.

Making a DNA Fingerprint

The first step in making a DNA fingerprint is to extract DNA from blood, hair, or other cells. In the more common method of fingerprinting, the DNA is then mixed with chemicals called enzymes. The enzymes cut a DNA molecule into shorter pieces. Each time the enzymes come across a certain sequence of nitrogen bases, the DNA molecule is cut. For example, one kind of enzyme cuts the DNA after every GGCC sequence. In this way, a long DNA molecule is broken apart into pieces of different lengths.

Next, the pieces of DNA are grouped by size by placing similar lengths of DNA next to each other. To do this, the DNA pieces are placed in a tray of gel. An electrical current is used to move the fragments. The current moves the shorter, lighter fragments faster than the longer, heavier fragments. Thus the shortest fragments move farthest across the gel and can be grouped together.

The next step is to look for specific sequences of nitrogen bases. The fragments are placed on a nylon sheet and marked with radioactive labels. A radioactive label is a chemical that sticks to a certain nitrogen base sequence. For example, one radioactive label might stick to the TAG sequence. Another label might stick to the CAT sequence. Then the nylon sheet is placed on X-ray film to make a picture. A dark band appears at every radioactive label, showing the position of the labeled DNA sequences. Usually the fragments are treated with four to six different labels to show several different sequences. A finished fingerprint resembles the bar codes used in a grocery store.

Once the fingerprint is done, the base sequences of two fingerprints are compared to see if the samples show the same or different patterns. If one DNA

Scientists examine an image of a DNA fingerprint.

sample is old or contaminated, it may not be possible to tell if the fingerprints are the same or different.

Fingerprints Point the Finger

Using DNA fingerprints, detectives have solved crimes that had previously been unsolved. For eighteen years the FBI searched for a man known as the Unabomber. From 1978 to 1996, his bombs killed three people and injured twenty-three others. Some of his bombs were sent through the mail. The FBI searched and searched for the Unabomber, but could not determine his identity.

Finally the Unabomber's brother recognized his writings from an article the Unabomber sent to newspapers. The FBI now suspected Ted Kaczynski as the Unabomber. In 1996 they raided Kaczynski's cabin in Montana. There they found many things that pointed to Kaczynski as the bomber. Bomb-making materials, clothing that matched descriptions of the bomber, the original copy of his newspaper article, and a typewriter were seized as evidence.

One piece of evidence came from the Unabomber himself. The stamps from the Unabomber's letters were sent to a laboratory for DNA fingerprinting. The laboratory analyzed the DNA from the saliva on the back of the stamps. They found that it matched Ted Kaczynski's DNA fingerprint. The Unabomber was convicted of his crime and sent to jail.

The infamous Unabomber Ted Kaczynski (center) is led to court for trial. DNA fingerprinting proved he was responsible for a series of deadly bombings.

Innocent or Guilty?

DNA evidence often helps convict criminals. More often, however, DNA fingerprints prove that a suspect did not commit a crime. In 1992 two lawyers founded the Innocence Project. Their aim was to help people who were in jail win their freedom if they were innocent. They also wanted to prevent innocent people from going to jail.

The Innocence Project takes cases where DNA fingerprints show that a person did not commit a crime. Sometimes DNA evidence was not available when a person went to trial. In some cases a DNA sample was lost or mislabeled. Some people are misidentified as criminals by a witness. In its first ten years the Innocence Project used DNA evidence to prove more than 120 people who were in jail were innocent.

In 1989 a twenty-eight-year-old jogger was brutally attacked in New York's Central Park. The jogger

Kirk Bloodsworth (center), the first person released from prison based on DNA testing, watches as the Innocence Protection Act is unveiled in Washington, D.C.

survived but could not remember anything about the attack. Police arrested five teenagers for the crime. After the teens were questioned for many, many hours, they confessed to playing a part in the crime. The teens were convicted of the crime even though their stories were all different. In 2002 a convicted criminal admitted that he alone committed the crime. All of the DNA evidence from the crime scene matched his DNA fingerprint. None of the DNA evidence matched the five teens. The convictions of the wrongly accused teens, now grown men, were overturned.

Because of DNA fingerprints, detectives can now eliminate many suspects before a trial. In the future, DNA fingerprints may be used routinely to accurately identify people.

Chapter 4

Cloning

Identical twins look alike because they have the same genes. Identical twins start to develop in the same way as a single baby. A sperm fertilizes an egg. The genes from both sperm and egg combine, forming an embryo. But soon after fertilization, the growing embryo splits in two. Each of the two embryos develops into a baby with identical genes. Because each baby has the exact same genes, identical twins are **clones** of one another.

Many plants make clones. A strawberry plant sends out long stems that grow across the surface of the ground, called runners. New plants grow at the end of the runners. Each new plant has an exact copy of the original plant's genes, so the plants are clones.

Today scientists can clone animals in laboratories. Starting with a single cell from an animal, they can create a new animal that is an exact genetic copy. This process is called **reproductive cloning**. Using reproductive cloning, animal breeders hope to pass on the genetic strengths from their best animals to the cloned animal.

Some scientists use cloning as a tool that may someday help them find cures for diseases.

How to Clone a Sheep

① DNA is removed from the egg of a sheep, and then placed in a culture medium.

② A cell from the sheep to be cloned is placed in a culture medium with the egg.

Original sheep

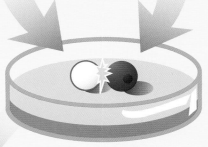

③ The egg and cell are joined together using an electrical spark.

④ The joined cell divides and forms an embryo.

Cloned sheep

⑤ The embryo is placed into host mother's womb.

⑥ The host mother gives birth to a clone of the original sh

Instead of cloning an entire plant or animal, they are hoping to clone different kinds of tissues and organs grown from single cells. This type of cloning is called **therapeutic cloning**.

Dolly

In 1997 Dolly the sheep captured the attention of the world. She was the first mammal cloned from only one parent. Prior to this time, a single embryo had been split in a laboratory to create two identical animals. The twins were clones of each other, but they had DNA from both of their parents. Dolly's genes were identical to her one parent.

Dolly the sheep was created as part of a Scottish research project whose goal was to produce valuable drugs to treat cystic fibrosis. The researchers put genes in sheep that caused them to make milk with a special protein. This protein is useful in treating cystic fibrosis. The researchers wanted to clone the genetically changed sheep. In this way they would produce more sheep that made milk with the special protein.

To create Dolly, a Scottish researcher named Dr. Ian Wilmut started with a sheep egg. He removed the nucleus from the egg cell, so the egg had no DNA. Then he took a cell from an adult sheep and combined it with the egg cell without a nucleus. He added a protein that made the cells fuse. The new egg cell had an exact copy of the adult's DNA.

Dr. Wilmut then gave the cell a jolt of electricity. The electricity made the cell start to divide and form an embryo. The embryo was transplanted into another sheep. The embryo developed normally, and Dolly was born.

Some people thought that because an adult cell was used to create Dolly, she would age prematurely. Dolly did start to show signs of aging when she was only five years old, even though sheep normally live to be about fifteen years old. Then the famous sheep died of a lung disease when she was six years old. However, there was no evidence that cloning was the reason for her death.

Dr. Ian Wilmut feeds Dolly, the first mammal cloned from only one parent.

Reproductive Cloning

Since Dolly's cloning, sheep, pigs, cows, goats, mice, cats, hens, and mules have been cloned in laboratories around the world. Cloning is a complicated process, and most of the egg cells fail to develop into animals. Of the animals that have been cloned, many have had genetic defects and health problems. Cloned animals have suffered from heart and lung defects, growth problems, and have been unable to fight off diseases. Some have developed normally, and then died suddenly. Some scientists believe that the DNA in adult cells works differently than the DNA in sperm and egg cells. Because of this, cloned animals have not been healthy.

Still, interest in cloned animals continues. DNA banks have been set up where people can store the genes of a favorite pet for future cloning. Some researchers suggest that endangered animals may someday be cloned.

While many people accept animal cloning, human cloning is more controversial. People worry that a cloned human would have genetic defects or other serious health problems. How would people decide whom to clone? Some people might want to clone only geniuses. Others might want to clone themselves because they want a child that is exactly like them. There may be legal problems about who is the parent of a cloned child. In some countries, laws have been passed to prevent research on human cloning.

Some day people may have their pets cloned.

A company named Clonaid claimed to clone human children in 2002. However, the company did not show proof of any baby cloned from a single parent. Without evidence, scientists did not believe the company's claims.

Therapeutic Cloning

Some cloning researchers are not trying to create genetically identical individuals. Instead, they hope to use cells from cloned embryos to cure diseases.

Diseases can harm human organs. Sometimes a person has a heart or lung or liver that does not work because of a disease. If a donor organ can be found, doctors try to transplant it into a patient's body. However, a person's body recognizes a transplant organ as something that does not belong to him or her. A transplant patient is given drugs so that the new organ will not be rejected. Often the patient's body still rejects the new organ.

Transplant organs may someday be grown from **stem cells**. Stem cells are cells from an embryo. These cells have not yet become specialized. As an embryo grows, its stem cells eventually turn into heart, lung, skin, nerve, or other types of cells. Once a cell is specialized, it does not grow into anything else. But stem cells have the potential to grow into any kind of cell, so they could be used to grow a variety of body parts.

Someday scientists may be able to create tissues and organs from a patient's own cells. Starting with a single cell from a patient, they would first clone an embryo. Using stem cells from the cloned embryo, they would grow the specific kind of tissue or organ that a patient needed. The new organs would not be rejected because they would have the same genes as

Patients at a hospital play basketball from their wheelchairs. Some day therapeutic cloning may help them walk again.

the person's cells. A sick person might not have to wait as long for a new kidney or heart or other organ.

Researchers are now trying to learn what causes a stem cell to grow into a certain type of cell. Understanding this might also help people understand why some cells may change and become cancerous cells. This could someday lead to the prevention of some types of cancer. Using stem cells, researchers also hope to grow healthy cells that will treat diseases like diabetes or Parkinson's disease.

Glossary

chromosomes: Strands of DNA found within the nucleus of every cell. Humans have twenty-three pairs of chromosomes.

clones: Cells, organs, embryos, or organisms that have identical genes.

DNA: Deoxyribonucleic acid, the chemical substance that contains genes.

DNA fingerprint: A picture that shows the sequence of some sections of DNA. A DNA fingerprint can be used to identify someone.

dominant: A form of a gene that always expresses itself.

genes: The basic unit of heredity that gives instructions to cells. Genes are passed on from parents to offspring. Each gene has instructions for one trait.

gene therapy: Medical treatment in which healthy genes are given to a person with defective genes that cause a disease.

inherited: A characteristic that is passed from parent to offspring.

mutation: A change in a gene.

nitrogen base: One of four chemicals in DNA that link in a specific order. The four kinds of bases are adenine, thymine, guanine, and cytosine.

protein: Chemical compounds that direct reactions inside a cell or make body structures. Proteins are made of amino acids.

recessive: A form of a gene that is expressed only when the organism has inherited two copies of it.

reproductive cloning: Creating organisms that are genetically identical to a single parent.

stem cells: Unspecialized cells from an embryo that have the potential to become many different types of cells.

therapeutic cloning: Cloning as a tool to help cure diseases.

trait: A physical characteristic that is inherited.

For Further Exploration

Books

Billy Aronson, *They Came from DNA*. New York: Scientific American Books for Young Readers, W.H. Freeman Company, 1993. Aliens discover the mystery of what makes Earth creatures who they are. An imaginative introduction to DNA and its role in living things.

Fran Balkwill, *DNA Is Here to Stay*. Minneapolis: First Avenue Editions, 1994. Using cartoon illustrations to demonstrate important concepts, this book introduces chromosomes, the genetic code, and the double helix.

Richard Beatty, *Genetics*. New York: Raintree/ Steck-Vaughn, 2001. An introduction to genetics, including modern genetic research and possible future uses of genetics.

Norbert Landa and Patrick A. Baeuerle, *Ingenious Genes: Microexplorers*. New York: Barrons Juveniles, 1998. An introduction to how genetic engineers copy and change genes to make plants and animals more resistant to diseases.

Cynthia Pratt Nicolson, *Mysterious You, Baa! The Most Interesting Book You'll Ever Read About Genes and Cloning*. Toronto: Kids Can Press, 2001. A well-written, engaging introduction to genes and heredity, including many modern and future uses of genetics. Highly recommended for young readers.

Internet Source

Dolan DNA Learning Center, "DNA from the Beginning, an Animated Primer on the Basics of DNA, Genes, and Heredity," 2002. www.dnaftb. org. Well written and illustrated with accurate, easy-to-understand information. Includes up-to-date links for each concept.

Index

mutations, 15–18, 19–20

nitrogen bases
    in DNA fingerprints, 27–29
    function of, 16
    pairs of, in cystic fibrosis
        gene, 19–20
    types of, in DNA molecule,
        25

pea plants, 8–10
physical features. *See* traits
plants
    breeding of, 6–7
    clones of, 33
    number of chromosomes
        and, 11
premature aging, 36
proteins
    building of, 19–20
    gene therapy and, 22, 35
recessive traits, 9, 10

reproduction, 14, 33
reproductive cloning,
    of humans, 37–38
    problems with, 37

sickle-cell anemia, 20
stem cells, 39–40
strawberry plants, 33

therapeutic cloning. *See*
    cloning, therapeutic
thymine (T) base, 25
traits
    dominant, 9, 10
    inheriting of, 6, 7–8
    of pea plants, 8–10
    recessive, 9, 10
transplant organs, 39

viruses, 21

Wilmut, Ian, 35–36

Picture Credits

About the Author

Buffy Silverman writes about the natural world from her home in Michigan. She is the author of two other books for young readers, *Bat's Night Out* and *Birds.* She has written many magazine articles for *Ladybug, Spider, Cricket, Highlights, Odyssey,* and *Ranger Rick* and writes items for educational publishers and testing companies. She is also a writing instructor at the Institute of Children's Literature. Buffy shares her home with her husband, biologist Jeff Conner, and their children, Jake and Emma.